chop

a collection of kwansabas for fannie lou hamer

treasure shields redmond

co-winner of the Rustbelt Appa/Affrilachian Midwest chapbook contest

winged city chapbooks

stow, ohio

Winged City Chapbooks
an imprint of
Argus House Press
Stow, Ohio

chop, a collection of kwansabas for fannie lou hamer

Printed in the U.S.A.

First edition, 2015
ISBN 978-1-943849-54-3

original cover art by Frank D. Robinson
cover design by Teneice Durrant
author photo by Kim Love

www.argushousepress.com

chop

a collection of kwansabas for fannie lou hamer

Dedication

Yaa Asantewa Williams, a free woman of color
To Eugene B. Redmond Ark/eye/tech
of the kwansaba

Acknowledgements

"around the time of medgar," "jericho," and "from my parlor window, 1964." *The Sou'wester* 39.2. (Spring, 2011) 30-32

"October 16, 1917, Montgomery County, Mississippi," "makn ends meet," and "chop." *Sententia* 4. (Winter, 2012) 122-124

table of contents

Why the Kwansaba?

I chose the Kwansaba through which to channel Mississippi's proto-womanist Black activist/organizer, Fannie Lou Hamer because the brevity of the form mirrors the shots of bourbon strong imagery that I hoped to convey. Each poem pushes forward an "aint it the truth" moment from the perspective of Hamer, and some of the other family members who witnessed her genius.

The form, created by poet Eugene B. Redmond is "In general . . . a praise song to a person, a principle, or an event." Even though it is true that the poems "praise" Hamer's accomplishments, they aspire to do much more. They also collude with the seven lines/seven words stricture in order to give homage to Hamer's southern charismatic Christianity (the same sort in which I was raised) that says "seven is God's favorite number." Finally, like many of Dickinson's masterpieces or Berryman's *Dream Songs* the poems seek to work in concert using the economical nature of the Kwansaba form to get at what was most essential about Hamer's mammoth contribution to American life.

Who was Fannie Lou Hamer?

When one thinks of the millions of souls lost during the transatlantic slave trade, the missed potential immediately jumps to mind. All genocide robs us of the few geniuses that each culture produces. At the beginning of the previous century the pernicious system named Jim Crow served as another sort of genocide in the U.S. A genocide of potential. Many scholars have written of the number of lynchings during Jim Crow, perhaps the most famous one being Ida B. Wells's *A Red Record*. Along with the incomprehensible loss of life, however, are the people who lived, but not really. The ones who weren't fortunate enough to die. Those who lived believing a system that counted them as less valuable, less competent, less human; that this system was right, godly, and, (maybe worst of all), unchangeable. When young people from the Student Nonviolent Coordinating Committee walked across a Cottonfield in 1962 they didn't know they were about to ignite one of the greatest intellects of the 20th century. Fannie Lou Hamer was born in 1917 in Sunflower county. She was a black woman. She was her mother's 20th child. The first half of her life was lived quite unremarkably. She was a churchgoing woman who married, raised two daughters, and through pure savvy and hard work, rose to the ranks of time keeper on her plantation. Mrs. Hamer joined the movement for civil rights without so much as a second thought, at the age of 44. She was known to reply to those who thought she should worry about being killed, that "[Jim Crow] had been killing [her] a little bit everyday" [of her life]. Mrs. Hamer went on to challenge the sitting Democratic Party in Mississippi, to run for numerous offices, to become a valued member of Martin Luther King's cadre of movement soldiers, to offer her very beaten body as evidence that Jim Crow had tried but not succeeded in killing her most radical self. These poems are my love letter to Mrs. Hamer, and every black woman like her who raised me in Mississippi, and who, for me, were not exceptional. With these poems I am exposing to the world, in much the same way the young people from SNCC did, that genocide is overwhelming, but it is not total. Beneath the shrapnel of Jim Crow lay undetonated intellects --working, serving, and keeping time, until they explode.

-Treasure Shields Redmond 7/30/15

october 16, 1917, montgomery county, mississippi

boss say i birthd twenty field hands
then givd me fifty dollars for fannie.
done promise this last one to god.
dream i givd her to the priest.
took her behind the holy of holies,
came out full grown and singn glory.
shook me woke. knowd i been changd.

makn ends meet

juke joint aint church; though prayr savd
me and paps from plain greens, flour
gravy, pig's ears, feet, snout. blues aint
christ-like til they fill bellies burstn
with home brew, moon shin'n through mason
jars like gold teeth against black lips,
greasd. skillets testify: faith fries, with work.

chop

yam on stove, water jug ready, spicket
bath, rag tied. groggy hands can't be
no stumbln block. nor suckln babe to
tend. sun be waitn his turn, watchn
me beat him to field. cotton is
calln. if five hundred pounds mean a
bale, how negroes be called “no count”?

ears and fingers

aint babies' ears and fingers sweet? bare
foot winters harden they feet; ashy elbows,
and scabbed knees grow callous. not them
ears and fingers. pretty fat thumbs, lobes
with baby hair still on 'em. mobs
even crave'em. pickld tokns, floatn cute
as can be in big store windows.

redish’

bus bound for indianola, full with colord
bodies. cotton choppd heads full with freedom
lessons. “be polite. eye contact. talk up.”
we aint wrong. we just know better.
extra shoes and my own freedom pen.
we gon' redish today. gon' redish today.
gon' redish today. we gon' redish today.

boss say she can come back

marlowe say: *she can come back, just*

take her name off that voter roll.

back to field. back to cabin. *back*

slidn is a sin, i say. back

to slopjar. back to thinkn rights was

flies -- been shoo'n them when i shouldv

been invitn them home for freedom supper.

poll tax

weren't right how they did us. wouldn't
kick no dog that ain't barkn' hell,
i was 44. told that doctor 34.
auntie, we just gone make it so
you don't be bothered with eve's curse,
he say. i votes for them babies.
babies that won't never stand in line.

around the time of medgar

first beatn was in a hot winona
jail. corn whiskey paid to a colord
man. beat me till he give out.
beat me like they told him. beat
my hips for bein' wide, my back
for not being bent. they beat us
all for the look in our eyes.

favorite verse

"whose hatred is covered by deceit, his wickedness shall be showed before the whole congregation." proverbs 26:26

script and verse i told the jailer's
wife. she bring lunch for her man.
i tell her bread of life hath
made one blood. her man drew blood,
do dirt behind bars. proverbs prove it
will come to light. " i been born
again," she say. lady, *read* your bible.

justice

we stay in holly springs. can't stay
in oxford. awaitn trial like daniel. den
so loud we hear it 25 miles
away. sheriff, police, highway patrol namd law
breakr. they got cousins in the jury
box, show'n they lion teeth; eyes shut
tight to this little light of mine.

white or colord

young folks argue into dawn bout whether
whites can work down here along side
colord . i done washd, cookd, caught they
babies. always behind or below. nevr beside.
my body broke for three days over
this debt. the spirit makes me ask:
aint it time they shared this cup?

my part

between kennedy and four little girls lay
mississippi. between texas sniper and georgia terror
stretch delta dust. wedged inside history. mingld
in medgar's bloody carport. i stand ready
to fall five foot four inches into
freedom. cock's crow won't signal denial out
my mouth. i'll take up the cross.

freedom summer

i prepare them best i can. tell
about the white man's deep fear; afraid
of payback cause he deserve it. we
need their bodies. young bodies from good
homes -- white bodies -- the kind folks can't
stand to see broken. israel done come
out of egypt. freedom summer done come.

from my parlor window, 1964

hate throw'n water on their fire. white
and colord holdn hands, going to town.
their clear eyes show me what could
be. see 'em under my pecan tree?
pointn at clouds, elbows touchn. shamed folks
into livn like the christ they claim.
do they daddies know they *this* free?

pap's blues

black balled is how they call it.
any colord redish', subject to get put
off the land. these crackers won't give
a crippld crab a crutch. now martin
king send a check every month. freedom
is fannie's trade. i aint got to
work. so i work on this bourbon.

jericho

johnson calld me “ignornt”. while he can't
see what's wrong in mississippi. then throw
a party, where half the childrn aint
invitd. the word say: my mansion is
in heaven. but before i get there
we might march around 'lantic city 7
times. bring a white house tumbln down.

is this america?

they call it a hear'n, but don't
nobody listen. too busy tryn to dickr
with the devil. i tell 'em what
god loves. see tears in they eyes.
what is they cryn for? colord done
cried an ocean. prayd enough to fill
a bible. now we want freedom. now.

3 ways til sunday

fannie, annie and vickie, three ways til
sunday. vickie hailing from forrest county. annie
raisd in madison. bear'n empty tomb witness
2000 years later. we roll away stone
for america. show 'em what's missing. i
loves these women. they accept my coarse
cloth. make a coat of many colors.

not be moved

we didn't come all this way for
no two seats. we make our stand
here on the old side of the
country. we saw these shores first. now
we come full circle. show you our
tree roots. shall not be moved. shall
over come. bent but not brokn. amen.

guinea, west africa – 1964

blacker than the tar i was always
told they would boil me in. i
was caught up in toure's white robe
like we gon' be caught on jubilee
day. he kissd me on both jaws!
put a ring on my prodigl hands.
now can you imagn johnson doin that?

malcolm

heard me sing freedom; tell about marlowe
kickn me off the job; about winona
jail. mr. x, with his red self,
preached white folk's funeral; eye for eye
and they sittn in the front row.
said he didn't feel like a man
when he heard how they beat me.

hard hearted

not when your rivers turnd bloody; not
when mlk's truth thundrd; not even when
your son fell in texas. now we
frog jumpn through your red dc. got
us a “moses” and a “aaron.” couldn't
stop now if we wanted to. freedom
like fire shut up in my bones.

preachers

chickn eatn preachrs. tom fool colords. we

have to watch them. this fire done

caught hold. tend to it like your

field. we all eat off what grows

here. can't have no coon stealn tendr

plants before they time. we almost there.

just keep your hand to the plow.

head start

po childrn don't see nobody like them
in the pre primer. see dick eat
dirt? see jane chop cotton? look at
jane's feet. do she cut the toe
off her shoes when they get too
small? do her hands crave a pencil
but make do with a dull stick?

vietnam

"If this is a GREAT SOCIETY I'd hate to see a bad one"

some get live sons back. some get
dead flags, tucked tight as a preachr's
grip. live ones come home full of
hell; wasted minds mostly still over seas.
what i could do with them soldiers
in sunflower county. how shall we sing
the lord's songs in a strange land?

paris green

poison put in my daddy's trough killd
our cow dead as a preachr in
memphs. murdrd our mule with paris green
envy ugly as 3 lynchd boys. here
lately the mob looks like us. stirrd
up in our food till we can't
tell what's good from what is poison.

little member

the word say this little tongue can
make big trouble. i use simple words:
free, land, free, medicne. they push back
with big words: marxist, social, exprmnt. just
one little woman talkn, will raise cain.
never met karl marx, but i know
a good idea when i hear one.

bound

my man paps wants to save me
up like change but this thick black
body is spent. spare breast. spare kidney,
fibrous womb taken fore i knowd it
was. gone lay down my burden. i'm
river side bound for the promise, god
i would serve him till i die.

About the Author

A native of Mississippi, Treasure Shields Redmond is a St. Louis metro-based poet, performer, and social justice educator. She most recently featured at the Nuyorican Poets Café. She has published poetry in such notable anthologies as *Bum Rush the Page: A Def Poetry Jam, Breaking Ground: A Reader Celebrating Cane Canem's First Decade* and in journals that include *The Sou'wester* and *The African American Review.* Treasure has received a fellowship to the Fine Arts Works Center, and her poem, "around the time of medgar" was nominated for a 2011 Pushcart Prize. A Cave Canem fellow, who has received an MFA from the University of Memphis, Treasure divides her time between being an assistant professor of English at Southwestern Illinois College and doctoral studies at Indiana University of Pennsylvania.